OH NO COLORING BOOKS

CALM AS F*CK

ADULT COLORING BOOK

30 Swear Words and Colorful Phrases

WARNING:
This coloring book is not to be taken seriously as it is calming as fuck.
Some have complained of having better days after filling in the
pages and even enjoying themselves while laughing with friends.
Please consult your doctor to see if you are healthy enough to
feel calm as fuck and/or to stop giving a shit entirely.

CALM AS F*CK ADULT COLORING BOOK

You Seem to Have Mistaken Me

for Someone Who Gives a Shit

LIFE ISN'T A GARDEN
SO STOP BEING A HO

COCKSUCKER

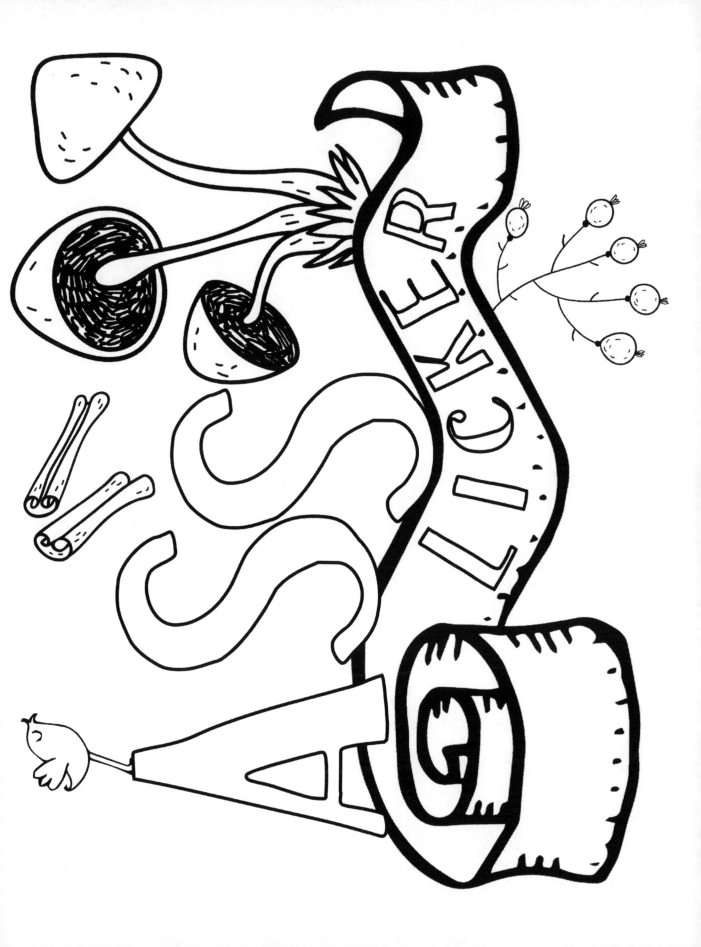

Don't you feel calm as fuck now?
Don't you?
If not, maybe take a deep breath
and slowly exhale until you feel calm and shit.

Feel it now?
Good.

Anyway, thanks for choosing this book. It means a lot.
If we sell more, maybe we'll start paying our new intern.
Maybe.
#SorryBecca.

Side note: we don't care about reviews.
We do care about coloring. It's fun. It's relaxing.
There are some shitbags in this world
who think that complaining is fun.
Why someone would be that
way is beyond us. That's why we don't care.
Color. Have fun. Don't be a shitbag :)

Want Free Coloring Pages?

Message us to sign up for our e-mail list:
(We'll send out free coloring sheets sometimes and NOT spam)
ohnocoloringbooks@gmail.com

Made in the USA
Lexington, KY
07 August 2018